D0955927

ALL THINGS ARE POSSIBLE

◇

SUE MONK KIDD

The C.R. Gibson Company • Norwalk, Connecticut 06856

Book design by John DiLorenzo
Typeset in Palatino
Cover design by Bob Pantelone
Cover photograph by Barbara Lans

Material in this book is reprinted from *Daily Guideposts*.
Copyright © 1979, 1980, 1981, 1982, 1983, 1984, 1985, 1986, 1988 by
Guideposts Associates, Inc., Carmel, New York 10512.

Published by the C.R. Gibson Company, Norwalk, CT 06856
ISBN 0-8378-1814-1
Printed in the U.S.A.
GB505

In quietness and in confidence shall be your strength.

Isaiah 30:15

◊

No matter how dark our pain, deep our failure, or difficult the obstacle in our way, we can find the strength not only to endure, but to overcome. For God has planted a power in the human heart that does not yield to darkness, a brave hope that with Him all things are possible.

I hurried along a narrow street in old Jerusalem. I took the steps that spiraled around a flat-roofed house into a large upper room. Inside a group gathered for a service. I stood in the back as the speaker began. My mind wandered to the day when a little band of shattered disciples had gathered in an upper room like this. Their Leader was dead, and they were plunged into despair. Suddenly, the words of the speaker caught my attention. "God is still at work," he said.

God is still at work! If only someone could have said that to the disciples that Saturday after the Crucifixion. They had huddled in the aftermath of defeat. And all the while the seconds closed in on the most staggering victory of human history. Though they couldn't see it...after they'd lost faith and walked away...God was still at work. At work on a victory far better than they could have dreamed.

In the room above Jerusalem, I thought of my own "Saturdays of defeat"–the days after a failure, the mornings after death, all those sequel moments to life's shattering events. And what had I done? I'd walled myself away, closeted in defeat and whimpered with my pain. The answer was the same for me as it had been for the disciples on that Saturday before Easter. Have faith. God is still at work.

This is a day for believing in the victories of your tomorrows.
Do you?

Cast thy burden upon the Lord, and he shall sustain thee.
Psalms 55:22

usk lay across the Garden of Gethsemane like soft gray velvet. I paused beside the gnarled trunk of an olive tree, remembering another night. Jesus had slipped into the garden, dropped to His knees, and grappled with the suffering He would soon endure.

Could that agonizing spot be close by? Even here, under this olive tree? As I looked beneath the tree, I saw the stem of a strange, ugly plant. It was covered with large thorns, sharp enough to tear a man's skin. I knew I was staring at the infamous "crown of thorns," the plant that had been curled into a cruel crown and shoved onto the head of Jesus before His death. Growing in the ground of Gethsemane, it was a prophetic picture of suffering, a symbol of all the agony Jesus endured. I wondered, *How did He bear so much?*

I stooped down and touched a thorn. As I did, I glimpsed something I'd almost missed. Near the ground a vibrant red bloom grew from the thorny stem. Not delicate, puny petals. This hateful "crown of thorns" grew a fiery little bloom.

I smiled to myself. Maybe that was the secret Jesus knew…that somewhere in every crown of suffering, God has implanted a bud of strength that can burst open, releasing an extra power.

This is a day for discovering God's strength. Have you looked for it within life's hardships?

Thou therefore endure hardness, as a good soldier of Jesus Christ.   II Timothy 2:3

Some time ago, I started a swimming program, beginning with only a few laps and intending to work up to a full mile of sixty-four, nonstop laps. But despite all my efforts, I could not get beyond twenty laps. It seemed that I had reached an invisible wall and now I was thinking about giving up. A mile seemed an utterly impossible goal.

As I slid into the water, another swimmer plunged in beside me and began her workout. Long after I had stopped, she swam up and down the pool. "Where do you get the endurance?" I asked.

"Once when I thought I couldn't possibly go another lap," she replied, "I somehow hung on for just one more. That was when I discovered my second wind. It was like shifting into a different gear that allowed me to go the distance."

I was fascinated. Was there really such a thing as "second wind?" The next time I hit my "wall" at twenty laps, I determined to hang on and to keep on swimming. Sure enough, I found a second wind! That was the day I reached the half-mile mark. Not long afterward I was swimming my "impossible" mile.

Is there a lesson here that can apply to my whole life? I think so. For when a problem rises up like a wall and it seems that I cannot go beyond it, I like to think of the second-wind capacity that God gave us. I am reminded never to give up too quickly; I seem to hear these energizing words of hope within myself: *"If you just hang in there a little longer, you'll make the distance."*

Lord, give us a determined spirit, a second wind,
when facing "impossible" situations.

And because of all this we make a sure covenant, and write it…   Nehemiah 9:38

ne day our Bible-study teacher handed out blue stationery to the class.

"I want you to think carefully and then write an 'I will' sentence," she explained. "Think of some goal you believe God wants you to accomplish, or perhaps something He wants you to overcome."

I stared at the paper for a long while. All sorts of questions surfaced in my mind. *What are my priorities? Where am I weak? What would God want me to overcome or accomplish?* Finally one thing became clear to me–an objective I knew God wanted me to reach for. So I scrawled it out, sealed my paper in the blue envelope, put my name on the outside and gave it back to the teacher.

As the days went by, I worked hard at my commitment, but soon the freshness and fervor faded. Two months later it was forgotten. Then, one month later, there in the mailbox was my blue envelope, inside of it the paper with my "I will" sentence. *Isn't she a wise teacher?* I thought. She had never opened our envelopes but had saved them for the moment when a commitment is apt to need its second wind. With that extra push, I was at last able to accomplish my goal.

If–like me–you need an extra portion of encouragement, why not place your spiritual resolution in a sealed, self-addressed envelope and hand it to a friend with a note that says, "Please mail this to me in three months."

Dear Father, help us to honor all our commitments to You.

Now unto him that is able to keep you from falling, and to present you faultless before the presence of his glory with exceeding joy…   Jude 1:24

ven after all these years I still remember the day in the third grade when I got back that terrible arithmetic paper. I had missed every single problem. Every one. I was so ashamed and angry with myself that I wadded up my paper and slumped down in my seat.

The teacher must have noticed my discouragement because she came over and put her arm around me and whispered, "It's not the mistakes you make that are most important, but how much you learn because of them." Then she smoothed out my crumpled paper. "Now try again."

I did. And that time my teacher wrote across the bottom of my paper, "IMPROVED."

That experience of my childhood is one that I hope I shall never forget. For I still make mistakes. Some of them cause me to feel ashamed and angry with myself. And sometimes when I am slumped down in guilt–berating myself–I can hear God whisper the same words in my ear: "It's not the mistakes that are most important, but how much you grow because of them."

I will never be perfect. But surely the next best thing is to be "IMPROVED."

Lord, may our failures and mistakes be
ground from which we may grow.

In quietness and in confidence, shall be your strength.

Isaiah 30:15

 t was the last round of the Master's golf
tournament. I stood pressed in the crowd
around the 15th green. Suddenly five
thousand heads turned in the same direc-
tion. Jack Nicklaus was striding down
the fairway. "When God handed out golf
talent, that man got an extra helping," said a man
behind me. How true, I thought, with a twinge of
envy.

Jack Nicklaus was a few shots off the lead. This
hole was crucial. Up in the fairway he planted his
feet over the ball. There was only one way to the
15th green: over a pond. Nicklaus swung. The
ball soared up, up, and suddenly it disappeared into
the water.

The gallery groaned. Nicklaus marched over and
looked down where the little white ball was under
half a foot of water. He untied his shoes, pulled off
his socks. Then he rolled up his trousers and waded
into the pond. The air was electric, Nicklaus was re-
fusing to give up a penalty shot. The crowd was
quiet. Nicklaus slashed his club into the water. For a
second he disappeared in a spray of water. Then I
saw the ball hurtling out of the water straight for the
pin. It touched down close to the hole. Nicklaus not
only saved par, he made a birdie.

Was it his "extra helping" of talent that did it?
Maybe. But it seemed to me the feat I'd just seen was
born more out of sheer, gritty determination than
anything else.

God gave me my own share of talent. Perhaps
what I need is not an extra portion of it, but some
gritty determination to make it soar.

*Father help us to roll up our sleeves and go to work
making the most of the talent You gave us.*

...Ye shall say unto this mountain, Remove hence to yonder place; and it shall remove; and nothing shall be impossible unto you.   Matthew 17:20

My daughter Ann loves the cartoon characters Garfield, the wisecracking cat, and Odie, the ever-cheerful dog. One morning she wanted to share a Garfield comic strip with me, but I was busy at my desk and waved her away. "Later, honey," I said, concentrating hard on the papers before me. The project I'd taken on was giving me trouble, and I was beginning to wonder if maybe I had bitten off more than I could chew.

Later that evening, Ann returned with her comic strip. It showed Garfield and Odie racing up the side of a tree and sitting on a limb, while below their owner protested, "Odie! Dogs don't climb trees."

"It's amazing what you can accomplish when you don't know what you can't do," observed Garfield.

The cartoon's message really got to me: Refuse to accept your limitations and those things you think you can't do, and you will be amazed at what you can accomplish.

No, I wouldn't drop the project that seemed so mountainous. With God's help, I would finish it in the spirit of Odie, who climbed a tree because no one ever told him he couldn't.

Lord, help us believe that with You all things are possible.

...But he that endureth to the end shall be saved.

Matthew 10:22

ne summer day I walked alone along Horseshoe Beach in Bermuda where great rocky boulders dot the shoreline, and I came upon a most unusual rock towering at the water's edge. There was a hole right through the center, so large that the rock resembled a hoop. *How peculiar,* I thought. *However did it get that way?*

I watched the water as it splashed upon the rock–wave after wave, spilling through the opening like a fountain. And then I understood. Water had worn the hole through the rock. Water! I knelt down to dip my hand into the surf, amazed that something as yielding and pliable as water could penetrate something as hard and unyielding as stone. What mystery and magic!

Yet as I saw the waves return again and again, I understood that it was not the *water* but the *persistence of the sea* that had made a way through the impossible. Arising, I continued on my walk, and I began to think of how easily I have sometimes given up on problems or dreams that seemed just too hard, too impenetrable. And there on the lonely beach it seemed that God had just reaffirmed to me one of life's most important truths. It *is* possible, with persistence, to make a way through barriers. Persistent prayer. Persistent love. Persistent hope. Persistent effort. The mystery and magic of overcoming very often lie in the simple art of keeping at it.

As the waves of the sea eternally return to the shore,
so do we return to You, Father.

"Whosoever shall smite thee on thy right cheek, turn to him the other also."   Matthew 5:39

W hen I was a little girl of nine or ten, one of my friends did not invite me to her slumber party.

I narrowed my eyes and poked out my lips. "I'll show her," I told my mother. "I won't invite her to *my* party."

"Maybe," Mother said, "there's a good reason why Alice didn't invite you."

Then she sat me down on her bed and told me this story. "Once there was a little girl who was walking along the sidewalk with her mother. After a while an old bulldog waddled toward them and stopped in front of the girl. The girl stared at the dog and, all of a sudden, stuck out her tongue, making a horrible face at him.

"Don't make ugly faces at the dog," scolded her mother.

"But he started it!" cried the little girl.

I giggled and interrupted my mother's story. And she smiled, too. Then she said, "See how silly it is to take offense at every ugly thing that comes your way."

I never did find out why Alice didn't invite me to her slumber party. But, thanks to Mom, she came to my next one, and I always went to hers after that.

When I've received a slight, Lord help me to give
a kindness in return.

Perfect love casteth out fear.

I John 4:18

◊

When we love, a mystery happens. The heart is set free from the confines of fear and we are opened more fully to people, to life and to the world. When we love, we are no longer afraid to see the beauty hidden in those around us, to reach out with a gesture of kindness or embrace the passion of living abundantly. Of all the mysteries in the universe, there is none more transforming and ablaze with joy than love. For wherever it is enacted, there is something of God.

Not long ago our old springer spaniel, Captain Marvel, had to have surgery. When I left him at the vet's, he looked at me with big, sad eyes. Back home I glanced at his quilt nestled on the carpet. He'd curled up on that old lap quilt day and night for years. It was where we knelt to scratch his ears and where he retreated after his baths. Remembering his sad look, I had a thought. *Carry Captain the quilt.* But it seemed like such a silly idea. Drive all the way back just to take a dog a quilt...the vet would think I'd lost my grip. Besides, I was very busy.

But Captain had washed the children's faces with sloppy kisses, pulled their wagon and chased their sticks for eleven years. I picked up the quilt and drove back to the vet.

I felt awkward handing it to the receptionist. But she smiled. (I think she'd seen my type before.) She left, then reappeared a moment later. "Poor dog's been crying all morning," she said. "But when I slipped the quilt in his pen, he curled up on it and closed his eyes."

That little quilt had made all the difference. And driving home, I had a new sense of just how important even the smallest gesture of love can be. I felt a prayer rising in my heart...

Oh, Father, help me take more time to love all Your creatures,
great and small.

Let all bitterness, and wrath, and anger, and clamor, and evil speaking, be put away from you...And be ye kind to one another, tenderhearted, forgiving... Ephesians 4:31, 32

 ne day when I was talking with my friend Ford about his childhood days spent on a chicken farm, he mentioned that chicken farmers had to trim the beaks of baby chicks. I didn't understand.

"There's a good reason," he told me. "You see, if one of the chicks falls and hurts itself, the other chicks peck at its wound with their sharp little beaks until the wound becomes much larger, even festering."

And I wondered then if sometimes we humans don't resemble the baby chicks. As when occasionally a fellow Christian falls, doing something we piously label "downright disgraceful." Don't some of us have a tendency then to peck away at the transgression–with gossip, tale-bearing, whispers of criticism and stares? The truth is that even one peck can deepen the pain, making the wound larger and less likely to heal.

Perhaps the farmers' solution is not such a bad one for us either. Jesus calls on us to "trim our beaks," so to speak–with compassion, forgiveness and kindness.

Should my neighbor slip and harm himself, Father, help me to contribute to the healing of his wound, not to the pain of it.

I t happened one day at the zoo. My daughter and I stood beside a grandmother and a little girl whose face was sprinkled with bright red freckles. The children were waiting in line to get their cheeks painted by a local artist who was decorating them with tiger paws.

"You've got so many freckles, there's no place to paint," a boy in the line cried. Embarrassed, the little girl beside me dropped her head.

Her grandmother knelt down next to her. "I love your freckles," she said.

"Not me," the girl replied.

"Well, when I was a little girl I always wanted freckles," she said, tracing her finger across the child's cheek. "Freckles are beautiful!"

The girl looked up. "Really?"

"Of course," said the grandmother. "Why, just name me one thing that's prettier than freckles."

The little girl peered into the old woman's smiling face. "Wrinkles," she answered softly.

That moment has whispered something to me ever since. If I look at others with the eyes of love, I will not see blemishes. Only beauty.

Help me to see beyond the "wrinkles" and "freckles"
of others to the loveliness within.

...Let us practice loving each other, for love comes from God and those who are loving and kind show that they are children of God...   I John 4:7

ot long ago I heard someone ask an elderly woman to express the secret of abundant living in the sunset years. I confess I never heard her answer for immediately my mind flashed to Mr. Card.

He was eighty when his first letter arrived. He'd met me, he said, through my writings. For six years his letters came once a month without fail. Warm letters about his farm, the Scottish music he loved, the spinning wheels he made in his workshop and the little country church where he'd taught Sunday school. Not once did he ever ask me to write back (though I often did).

Sometimes little presents arrived. A honey drizzle, homemade wooden toys for the children, a worn book, an old album of Scottish music, framed poems written in a familiar shaky scrawl.

One May, Mr. Card's family notified me of his death. But in June I opened the mailbox to find his familiar handwriting on an envelope. "By the time you read this," Mr. Card wrote, "I shall have gone on to my next great adventure. This last letter is to thank you for letting me love you..."

Today that letter—which he'd requested be mailed to me at his death—is a tender reminder that the secret to abundant living at any age is going through life asking, not how much do you love me, but rather, how much can I love you?

Lord, don't let me wait any longer or until it's too late; show me how to reach out to others in love now.

And after he had dismissed the crowds, he went up on the mountain by himself…   Matthew 14:23

y grandfather was a busy man, a judge who sat on the bench fifty years, an active churchman and community worker. But I also remember him fishing on the pond at his farm. At times he sat so long, he seemed to become one of those old mossy stumps along the bank. He would cast out the line on his cane pole, then lean back into the quietness. One evening, as the sun sank, I said, "Why don't you quit, Grandaddy? You haven't caught a fish all afternoon."

Grandaddy looked at the purple shadows creeping over the pond and said, "It isn't the fish I'm after, it's the fishing."

Some days when I find myself rushing around, more intent on producing results than I am on the glorious experience of being alive in the moment, I can hear his words floating on an old country breeze in my childhood. That's when I pause. I put the fuss and work aside, simply drop my line into the deep pool of the present moment and lean back into the quietness. For as my Grandaddy knew, "doing" is fine, as long as it's balanced with taking time to "be."

Lord, may my drive for "fish" never remove my joy of "fishing."

...As I have loved you, that ye also love one another.

John 13:34

ne afternoon, as my husband and I lay sunning on the beach, I noticed a middle-aged couple sitting on a towel with a poodle wedged between them. The man stroked the dog and absently gazed at the sea. The woman traced in the sand with her finger, from time to time cocking her head to see the effect. Later, when I looked again, they were holding hands.

The hours passed. The tide crept away. The couple with the dog left. My husband and I dragged the children from the water and headed back to the cottage. Passing the spot where the couple had sat holding hands, I noticed the woman's sand tracing. It read, *I love you*.

Three sandy words stared up at me—words that I was sometimes too complacent or too busy to say. And they reminded me of the need to put love into words. *I love you*. Simply saying the words...writing them...unleashing them...somehow makes life warm and special, full of potential. They had made a couple suddenly hold hands on a crowded beach...and feel cherished.

The waves broke into wide smiles across the shore. In the distance, the children danced after my husband and I chased after them...my heart full of the words on the sand, whispering...

I love you.

Notwithstanding the Lord stood with me, and strengthened me.
                                                    II Timothy 4:17

I have a vivid childhood memory of the day that my little brother Wade and I were playing hide-and-seek. He was hiding; I was seeking. After searching for a long time, I heard frantic, muffled cries coming from the bathroom. Finding the door locked, I hurried to tell my mother. She grabbed a kitchen chair, rushed outside and dragged it behind her across the grass. She placed the chair under the bathroom window and stood on it.

"The window screen is locked," Mother said with a note of desperation in her voice.

Then the strangled sound of Wade's cry filtered through the window. At that moment my mother, an average-sized woman, reached up with her bare hands and tore the sealed screen right off the window and wrenched open a steel lock. She climbed through the window and found my brother wedged inside the clothes hamper.

Mother never again equaled that incredible feat of strength. She did not ordinarily possess such power.

But the memory of my mother standing on the chair beneath the window gives me hope. I remind myself that no matter the problems life brings, God will give me the resources I need in order to cope—when the time comes.

Help us to live with the confidence that what we need to meet life's challenges, You will provide at the right time.

For God hath not given us the spirit of fear; but of power, and of love, and of a sound mind.   II Timothy 1:7

 hen my husband was seriously ill and undergoing surgery, I was filled with anxiety. "Oh, I'm so afraid!" I cried to a friend who waited with me.

She nodded and then gave me a knowing smile. "Do you know how many times the Scriptures say, 'Fear not,' or 'Do not be afraid'?"

I shook my head.

"It's a very curious number," she continued. "Three hundred and sixty-five times."

"But that's..."

"Yes, one for each day of the year," she said, finishing my sentence.

A coincidence? Perhaps. But I learned something then that I've never forgotten. God wants so much for you and me to get the message that He tells us over and over again–every day of our lives–"Fear not, I am here."

On that day in the hospital those words had a tremendous calming effect on me. And isn't it marvelous that we can turn to them for comfort at any time, on any day? They're always right there before us–on every page of the calendar–where they echo down through the years to gently ease our fears and our trials. All we have to do is claim them.

Help us, Father, to remember that we need never fear when we take Your hand.

Preserve me, O God: for in Thee do I put my trust.

Psalms 16:1

 **S**uddenly the drums rolled. My childrens' eyes sparkled. It was their first circus. High over the center ring, a high-wire artist on a bicycle prepared for a "death-defying" ride–without a net. Suspended from the bicycle was a bucket-like wagon. A daring young girl blew a kiss and climbed into the bucket. The children covered their eyes.

"Mama," Bob asked, "do you think he can pull her across?"

I patted his hand. "Sure I do."

He squinted nervously into the top of the tent. "I mean do you *really* believe it?" he asked.

"Yes, I *really* believe it." I assured him.

"But Mama," Bob said unconvinced, "would *you* get in the wagon?"

I fell silent, taken by surprise. That was altogether different.

A few weeks later I discovered a parable hidden there: A night when Bob was very sick. He tossed in a feverish sleep and coughed deep and hollow, making a frightening sound. I prayed for him, but still I was worried. A deadly flu was going around. As I sponged his wet, hot face, Bob's words came back to me like far off music on a gentle breeze..."Mama, do you *really* believe he can pull her across? Would you get in the wagon?"

And suddenly I knew. Faith was something more than words or a nice feeling. Faith was climbing into God's wagon and riding across the unknown place in life, without a net.

With an act of will I laid it all in God's hands. And sure enough, the three of us–me and God and Bob–reached the other side...safe.

Lord, give us daring faith.

"I am come that they might have life, and that they might have it more abundantly."   John 10:10

She was a friend of mine in college. Young and healthy. Yet she never went anywhere without a hot-water bottle and an umbrella. Evelyn was one of those people who seemed to hold the world at arm's length.

One summer day she went with me to a lake party. We arrived as the sun sprinkled its shining light onto the water like bobbing diamonds. I stood at the water's edge, taking it all in. Above, clouds floated in silence. The whole world seemed like a big, bright invitation from God.

Then I noticed Evelyn. She put up her umbrella against the sun, draped a scarf over her shoulders and was rubbing lotion on her legs. "Any bug spray?" she asked.

"Come on," I said. "Let's swim."

"The water looks murky to me," she replied. "Besides, my sinuses may flare up."

So I dove in without her. As I did, I saw Evelyn huddled on her towel, slapping bugs, not seeing or feeling the world. Not really involved in life.

My father called this "surface living." There have been times when I have fallen into its subtle trap. I gave in to inertia. I let the wonder dim and my awareness slip away. And instead of seeing a lake, I began seeing a hazard to my sinuses.

But Jesus spoke of abundant living. Maybe, in part, He was saying that He came to wake us up to the joys of existence, to coax us off our towels into involvement with life where we see all the world as God's miracle, and enter in.

Lord, help me take the plunge.

I t was one of those little skits put on by children. It lasted for only five minutes and I don't even remember what it was all about. I do remember, though, that my son wore a sign around his neck that read "Mr. Disagreeable."

All of the characters in the skit were impersonating certain human qualities. The lot of them paraded around–smirking, scowling, giggling–each trying his or her best to look the part.

The sight of my son with this sign hung around his neck made me pause and think. Do I label people with particular faults, tying the tags on them with double knots?

"You're so stubborn"…"You never listen to me"… "Why are you so careless all the time?"…

I had often said these things to my son. Suddenly, I saw my words as little signs, black-and-white yokes hung around his neck, bonding him to his weakness.

"Mama, untie the string." The skit was over and my son had backed up to me, wanting to be released from the sign. "You're free," I told him, slipping the string out of its knot. And I prayed that he would remain so.

The only sign that I will ever hang on him again is "Child of God."

O Father, help us to be sensitive to one another as You are to us.

I will go before and make the crooked places straight.

Isaiah 45:2

◇

Wherever we walk in life, whether through grief, uncertainty, worry or despair, there is One who not only travels with us in the present, but goes before us into the future, making the path straight. When the way grows crooked, watch with care. For that is when God appears like a mother's kiss or a spring of water breaking into a thirsty moment. We are never alone in our need.

I will not leave you comfortless: I will come to you.

John 14: 18

This was our last morning at the seashore. It was early and I stood gazing from the balcony of the little beach cottage. The vast ocean stretched before me. It seemed to roll across the whole earth, swallowing even the mightiest mountains in its wake. I shivered at the loneliness of its deep, shadowed depths.

A line of pelicans swooped low over the water and dropped like a single dipper into the sea. It was then that the familiar Bible verse surfaced from my memory: "If I take the wings of the morning and dwell in the uttermost parts of the sea, even there shall thy hand lead me and thy right hand shall hold me." *Even there!*

Yes, in every place of my life God is available, at any moment. Even here, with the vast, mysterious sea stretching before me, causing me to feel small and insignificant. No matter how deep a problem may be, or how shallow the need...*even there* God is with me. *Even there.*

The words echo deep within me–on lonely days, problem days or just plain ordinary days. On days when I'm far, far away from this beautiful, vast sea...*Even there...even there.*

Thank You, Lord, for the assurance that there is nothing in life that we need face without You...the most wonderful God-gift of all!

My little niece Laura died on a warm September day. She was four months old. When I arrived at my brother's home, my mother met me in the driveway, tears trickling down her face. Under the pine trees, we held each other.

"I'll be all right," she said finally, straightening up and brushing her cheeks. "Everyone says that time will heal this hurt."

"I'm sure it will," I replied, aware how feeble the words sounded.

Mother looked off into the distance. "I know it's foolish, but I find myself wishing it were next year already."

I've thought a lot about her words. When we come down into some valley of tragedy in our lives, we long for a bridge to get us to the other side so we won't have to walk through the pain below.

But to get to the healing side we must go ahead and dry the tears, experience the ache and struggle with the questions for which there are no answers. But there is also a promise to hold on to: "Though I walk through the valley of the shadow. . .thou art with me" (Psalms 23:4.) God goes down into the pain with us and helps us reach the other side.

A year has gone by since Laura's death. With God, Mother walked through the grief. Today, at Laura's name, she can smile without tears.

Lord, with You as our Rod and our Staff, we will walk through life's pain and problems without fear.

Come to me, all ye that labor and are heavy laden, and I will give you rest.

Matthew 11:28

A legend has it that there once lived a man of towering strength, a giant of a man. He was a pagan whose strength perhaps led him to believe that he needed no higher power.

He made his living by carrying travelers across a broad river. One day a child came to the river. As the man bent down to allow the child to climb upon his back, the lad said, "Are you sure you can bear my weight?"

The man laughed. "Why, I've carried full-grown men across this river. You, my little one, will be lighter than a pebble."

"Very well," said the boy. "But I must warn you. I am heavier than I look."

With a grin, the man raised the child upon his massive shoulders and stepped out into the swirling water. But the weight on his back grew strangely heavy. Soon the brawny giant was struggling.

With superhuman effort, he crawled up onto the opposite bank and let the child down.

"How can you be so heavy?" the perplexed man asked. "Who *are* you?"

"I am Jesus of Nazareth," replied the boy. "And I carry the burdens of the world on my shoulders. Let me carry yours, too."

And so, Christopher, today known as St. Christopher, was converted to Christianity. This story reminds me that I don't need to struggle across each day on my own. There is One stronger than I. He is the Great Burden-bearer and on his shoulders there is always room for one more.

Jesus, carry us through this day.

And God shall wipe away all tears from their eyes.
Revelation 7:17

 watched my three-year-old daughter from the window. Ann pedaled her shiny red tricycle down the cement driveway, around the blossoming magnolia, across a batch of dandelions, a left turn at the gardenia bush, gathering steam by the oak. I smiled at her little roadway. There were actually tricycle ruts there! I went back to my suitcase open on the bed and continued packing for a weekend trip with my husband. Then...a thud! A wail! A door slam! Ann burst into the room, in tears. She lifted a skinned knee. I knew exactly what she wanted. Not a bandage. But a kiss. We called it kissing the hurt. I bent down, dried her tears and placed a kiss on her knee. The makings of a smile appeared in her face and popped out in a giggle. In some secret, comforting way, the love in the kiss had made the hurt better.

Ann looked at the suitcase. "Who will kiss my hurts while you're gone?" she said. I was about to say the baby-sitter, when her face lighted up and she asked, "Mommy, does God kiss hurts?" I cupped her chin in my hand. "Yes, darling, God kisses hurts even better than mommies."

When the pain in life strikes, when the falls and failures come, when the lonely tears flow, remember: God is nearby with healing love and secret comfort. Go to Him. For He will surely bend down and kiss the hurt.

Lord, the hurts come.
But we find comfort in Your love.

Fear thou not; For I am with thee…I will strengthen thee; yea, I will help thee.   Isaiah 41:10

I was clipping rose blooms when I heard my daughter's small voice across the yard. "Give me back my doll."

Ann stood behind a young crabapple tree, staring at her older brother and his buddy. The boys had apparently snatched her doll from the stroller she'd been pushing around the backyard. They held the doll behind a stack of last winter's firewood. I also noticed my old pillow case nailed to a broom handle hanging over their "fort." On it was scrawled "Red Devils." Indeed! I thought.

"Come get her," they teased. But Ann clung to the slim tree, tears beginning in her eyes, unable to muster the courage to retrieve her doll.

Just as I started to intervene, my husband's car pulled into the driveway and Ann galloped to meet it. A minute later she showed up at the "fort" with her daddy right behind her. This time she stuck her chin out bravely. "Now give me my doll!" It was thrust into her hands instantly.

Standing behind the rosebush, I couldn't help but smile at what had taken place inside a little girl's heart because of the quiet, sure presence of her father at her side. She overcame her self-doubt and found her courage.

It can happen to you too. If today you face something that requires more strength and courage and coping ability than you feel you have, take heart. Your Father is right behind you.

Father, help us to draw upon Your quiet, sure presence
to unlock the resources within ourselves.

...I will go before thee, and make the crooked places straight...   Isaiah 45:2

e were cross-country skiing when we rounded a curve and found ourselves facing a frozen lake.

"Let's cut across," my husband said.

I studied the scene. The ice gleamed like a mirror. *Breakable?* I wondered. "Ski across a lake?" I asked. "What if the ice should give way?"

"I'll check it out," my husband replied. Gingerly he slid his skis out onto the ice, where they cut two silver ribbons behind him. "Solid," he announced. "Now stay right behind me. It will be safe *if you follow in my trail.*"

So we wound our way in a serpentine course out over the ice. Halfway across I had a sharp stab of doubt: *What am I doing out here?* My skis seemed to move slower and slower. I was not unlike Peter walking after Jesus on the Sea of Galilee, filled with doubt–and sinking.

"Come on," Sandy called, glancing back at me. I looked up at him and began to inch forward, following his trail in the ice. Gradually my doubts eased and I moved ahead with renewed confidence.

The little adventure taught me a lesson–one for those uncertain moments when life seems about to crack and give way beneath my feet. When my eyes focus only on the problem, I am apt to become immobilized. But when I concentrate on Jesus and *follow His trail*, my faith burns bright and I move steadfastly ahead. The lesson is as old as the Sea of Galilee but still true today. Jesus is always there, up ahead...leading the way.

When we are on thin ice, Lord, sustain us.

Heaviness in the heart of man maketh it stoop...

Proverbs 12:25

 t was 5:30 p.m. and I was peeling potatoes. My husband's car pulled in the driveway, his feet dragged through the door and his briefcase tumbled into the first chair.

"Hard day?" I asked.

"Just worried about some things at work," Sandy mumbled, his brows drawn into a tight frown.

"Why not take a nap before supper?" I suggested.

As he shuffled past me, I went back to my potatoes, feeling worried because he was worried.

I was on the last potato when I heard whistling coming from the back yard. I glanced through the window and there was Sandy, kneelng in his back-yard vegetable garden, whistling.

That's a switch, I thought. I sauntered out to the garden. "I thought you were taking a nap," I said.

"I decided I'd be better off pulling weeds," he said, motioning to a little pile of dandelions and crabgrass beside him.

I smiled, knowing just what he meant. Since then, when my mind grows tangled with worries, I try a method like his. I wander out to the garden and imagine my mind like the good fertile soil. And as I tug at a weed, I think of something that is bothering me. Pretty soon I have a little pile of uprooted worries beside me. Sometimes I stay in the house and go through my desk, throwing out the trash. There are all sorts of mindless tasks that I can find to weed out my worries. For worries are a lot like weeds, aren't they?

Help us to use our "down" moments creatively, Lord.

Behold, I am the Lord, the God of all flesh: is there any thing too hard for me?   Jeremiah 32:27

hen I was a child, my daddy took me to the ruins of a Civil War prison in the little town of Andersonville, Georgia. As we walked about the ghostly old walls, we came upon a stream of water bubbling from the ground through a wall. And there my daddy read me the true story of the stream as it was engraved on the historical marker above it.

During the war the inmates of Andersonville Prison ran out of water. Their only source had been a nearby stream, which became contaminated. With hope nearly gone, fourteen prisoners bowed their heads in prayer and asked God to send them water. And so it happened that a fresh, clean spring broke suddenly out of the ground and flowed through the prison. It still flows today. And the name of the spring is Providence.

I remember the awe I felt that day as I stood beside the mysterious silver spring. It reminds me that similar miracles can still happen. God comes like a spring of hope when things seem bleakest. And that is why you and I should never give in to despair. God *does* provide. Always.

Father, we are thirsty. Teach us to pray.

Behold, I make all things new.   Revelation 21:5

A morning sky arched over the little garden like a gray umbrella. I stood in a group of tourists at the garden's edge, beside a tall stone wall. We stared at the wall, joined in quietness. It was not an ordinary wall.

Hewn in the stone was a narrow door and inside a first century tomb...believed to be the tomb of Jesus. The onlookers filed inside, a solemn little procession. I stood back and looked at the wall. High up in the cracks of the stone were the wiry skeletons of a few dead bushes.

It was my turn to enter. I ducked my head and stepped into the hollow room. It was empty, chilled, dark. Suddenly I felt sad, sensing something of death's bleakness.

As I stepped out, I looked up, over my shoulder. Just above His tomb, bursting from a tiny crack in the cold, gray lifeless wall, was a cluster of shining clover. Living green clover! I couldn't imagine how I'd missed it going in, except that I'd been staring at the darkness through the door. Yet above...a clump of gentle clover. It haloed the door like a breath of life. It seemed to whisper, "There is life beyond this tomb. Step out. Look up. There is life!"

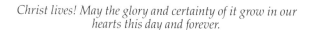

Christ lives! May the glory and certainty of it grow in our hearts this day and forever.

Pray one for another.

James 5:16

◇

The ways we pray for others are as varied and creative as the ways in which God answers. Whether we ask with boldness or listen in silence, we unleash an enormous power. Praying for others opens a channel through which God pours himself into the world. Prayer changes those for whom we pray. But mostly it changes the pray-er.

t a conference I attended, there was a woman who radiated a presence evident to almost everyone. People always gathered about her–automatically, it seemed. During a break I found myself talking with her about prayer. "Sometimes there is so little time for prayer in my life, for taking moments to be in God's Presence," I said.

"Do you read the newspaper?" she asked.

I nodded, wondering what the newspaper had to do with it.

"I've been combining the two for years," she said. "Each morning I carry out a spiritual exercise with the paper, and not only does it save time, but it enriches my prayer life *and* my reading."

Her method was simple. She began on the front page, praying for each event as she read. "Sometimes my heart is torn by all the tragedy, and I feel God hurting along with me for all His children," she said. "But there is also good news, and I thank God for each occurrence."

The local news was her "listening page," where she listened for any prompting God might give her– writing a letter about a council vote or carrying clothes to a needy family...

At wedding and birth announcements, she prayed for each marriage, each baby. At the obituaries, she prayed for families of those who had died. While smiling over the comic strips, she opened herself to God's healing through laughter.

"Do you think your prayers have made a difference in the world?" I asked.

"Oh, yes," she said. "But it begins with me..."

Father, each day we will pray through the pages of our newspapers listening for Your promptings and, we hope, making a difference in Your world.

One afternoon while doing research in the library, I came upon an odd sight. Sitting on a little stool in the stacks, a woman sat sound asleep. She sagged against the shelf, lines of exhaustion and worry drawn in her face. And suddenly a thought surfaced in my mind: *Pray for her.*

Having no idea of her needs, I simply envisioned her bathed in the light of Christ. I imagined it surrounding her on all sides, giving her new energy, life, joy, hope, insight–whatever she needed. Then I walked on.

Around the corner I saw a man studying a book. *Pray for him.* As I walked on, I lifted him into the light of Christ, too. Next there was a young mother... the librarian...a man at the card catalog. The adventure grew until I saw each person I came across bathed in the light of Christ, having a personal, unknown need met.

And I noticed something. Not only was I interceding for those around me, I was communing with God at the same time. In fact, it was one of the most God-conscious afternoons I'd ever spent. And it occurred to me that one of the best ways to keep my mind anchored upon God was by aiming prayers of light at those around me.

As I left the library and stepped into the stream of the street, I beamed a prayer at an approaching stranger, finding God's Presence fresh as the winter air.

Jesus, as we go about our normal activities every day, help us lift the people with whom we come in contact into Your light.

I exhort therefore, that, first of all, supplications, prayers, intercessions, and giving of thanks, be made for all men…
I Timothy 2:1

My son Kevin is going into the hospital two weeks from Monday," a friend said to me in the drugstore. "Please pray for him on that day."

"Of course," I replied. And as I walked away, I thought, *How many times have I said "Of course" and then forgotten? Well, not this time!* I took my calendar from my purse and penciled in Kevin's name across the top of Monday's page.

When the day rolled around and I consulted my calendar, as I do each morning, I was surprised to see Kevin's name. Aha! Once again I had forgotten. Without my diary reminder, the day would have come and gone without a prayer for Kevin.

Kevin became the focus of my prayers on that day. I prayed for him when I waited at stop lights, while I was at the dishwasher, when I was in the shower and as I waited in the schoolyard to pick up my children. Later, after I learned that Kevin was at home and successfully recuperating from his surgery, I realized how powerful that encounter with intercessory prayer had been. And so I began to pencil in other names on my calendar—my husband's name on the day he planned to travel, my son's name on the day he had a math test, a widow's name on the anniversary of her husband's death.

Now I know that a date calendar can serve as more than a reminder of daily activities. It can become a *prayer* calendar, bringing my loved ones and God into all the activities of my life.

Remind us, God, to pray for others
throughout the hours of our day.

ne Saturday morning while folding diapers I was struck with a mystifying thought: *Go see Miss Mulky.* Now I don't know when I'd thought of Miss Mulky. Why, I barely knew her. She was an elderly shut-in who lived a block away. The more diapers I folded, the more vivid the thought became. *Go see her!* At that moment the baby woke up crying, and my mind shifted to strained carrots and a warm bottle of milk. Miss Mulky was forgotten.

But as I sat in church the next morning, Miss Mulky popped right back in my mind while the choir sang. Was God trying to tell me something?

When church ended, I couldn't resist. I stopped by Miss Mulky's on the way home. "Thought I'd drop in for a visit," I said.

Miss Mulky smiled a knowing smile. "I've been asking God to send someone by. I need my heart pills refilled. I took the last one yesterday morning."

It was my turn to smile. "I know," I said. "It was while I was folding diapers."

God sometimes works with a little nudge, a message dropped into your thoughts, an idea springing from nowhere. Tune in and listen. God may be trying to tell you something.

Lord, when You speak, let us recognize Your voice.

And all things, whatsoever ye shall ask in prayer, believing,
ye shall receive.   Matthew 21:22

I t had been an hour since my husband had gone into surgery. I sat in the waiting room, suspended in that unbearable time when life dangles in uncertainty.

What if there's been a complication, I thought, twisting a button on my sweater. What if they found something awful?

Suddenly I could sit no longer. I paced across the room to the window. Next to it sat a woman, waiting as I was. Yet she sat there placidly reading. I glanced idly at the book she held in her hands, noticing a bookmark lying across the open page. On it, printed in a child's hand with red crayon, were the words—LIFE IS FRAGILE. HANDLE WITH PRAYER.

Why, of course, I thought, life *is* fragile. And there *is* a way to approach its most anxious moments.

I returned to the chair. "Dear Lord..." I began.

*Into Your gentle hands, dear Lord, we give our worries
—and ourselves.*

Not long ago I heard a story about a young man and an old preacher. The young man had lost his job and didn't know which way to turn. So he went to see the old preacher. He paced about the preacher's study and ranted about his problem. Finally he clenched his fist and shouted, "I've begged God to say something to help me. Tell me, Preacher, why doesn't God answer?"

The old preacher, who sat across the room, spoke something in reply–something so hushed it was indistinguishable. The young man stepped across the room. "What did you say?" he asked.

The preacher repeated himself, but again in a tone as soft as a whisper. So the young man moved closer until he was leaning on the preacher's chair. "Sorry," he said. "I still didn't hear you."

With their heads bent together, the old preacher spoke once more. "God sometimes whispers," he said, "so that we will move closer to hear Him." This time the young man heard.

We all want God's voice to thunder through the air with the answer to our problems. But God's is the still, small voice, the gentle whisper. And perhaps there's a reason. Nothing draws human focus quite like a whisper. God's whisper means I must stop my ranting and move close to Him, until my head is bent together with His. And then, as I listen, I so often get my answer. But better still, I find myself much closer to God.

From now on, Lord, we promise to listen more carefully.

The will of the Lord be done.   Acts 21:41

ne spring during routine surgery my husband lost his voice. He woke from anesthesia speaking in a raspy whisper. We were told it was inadvertent nerve damage–permanent and irreparable. I remember the cold, numbing shock that sliced through me. To my husband his voice was like hands to a surgeon. He was a minister.

For months, every time I watched him struggle to be understood, I would pray, "Please, God, give us a miracle. Give him his voice." Every time I saw him unable to call the children or sing his silly songs, I would ask for a miracle.

A year passed. I prayed. I pleaded. But there was no miracle. His voice did not return. My husband went on with his ministry. But this handicap that had changed our lives imprisoned me like a wall. I kicked at it till I was exhausted.

One morning I buried my head in my arms and cried, "Lord, for one year I've asked for a miracle. Where is it?"

The mail came early that day. There was a letter from a college teacher I'd not heard from in eight years. Out fell an orange sticker, as small as a postage stamp. On it was a gull, its wings spread in flight. And below it, these words, "There is a miracle inside you."

I knew then that God had spoken in His wise and gentle way. When there is no miracle to change the outward circumstances, the miracle must come from within…to accept what cannot be changed.

With God's help I began to accept. And like the gull, I found new freedom.

Thank You, Lord, for the miracle that lies within us,
the miracle of acceptance.

T he room was still. The five of us had been praying and sharing together. "Let Your will be done in our lives, Father," the newest member of the group prayed. Several silent moments enfolded the group and then another member cleared her throat. I knew exactly what she was going to pray.

For years Janie had lived with what she felt to be a terrible injustice. Her brother had manipulated their father's will so that he received the bulk of the inheritance. They had hardly spoken since. But gradually she recognized this breach was not God's will and prayed that God would impress upon her brother his wrong and help him find the courage to come and seek her forgiveness. She waited, but months passed and her brother never came.

One day she shared her prayer for God's will with the old housekeeper who had taken care of her father before he died. "I know His will shall be done in time," Janie said.

The housekeeper, with the lined face of one who had known difficulties, replied, "Dearie, the will of God is a fine thing. But you don't wait for it as much as you join in the doing."

Of course it was hard for her to go to her brother. How did she know he would even listen to her? Eventually she went. Finally God's will was done and the two were reconciled.

Most of us in the prayer group knew the story. And just as I knew she would, Janie added her postscript to our prayer for God's will to be done. "And Father, let us be part of the doing," she whispered.

What can we do this day to help bring about Your will, Father?

For with the heart man believeth unto righteousness; and with the mouth confession is made unto salvation.

Romans 10:10

A proud young fellow walked into the village blacksmith shop just after the smithy had tossed a red-hot horseshoe on the ground to cool. Noticing it lying there, the young man bent down and picked it up...only to drop it in all haste.

"Kind of hot, isn't it, son?" asked the blacksmith.

"No, not hot," said the fellow, hiding his burned fingers. "It just doesn't take me long to look at a horseshoe."

I've done that–made a mistake and then been too proud to admit it. Jesus said that we all sin. We all burn our fingers. The trouble comes when we allow pride to prevent us from confessing the wrongs we do.

How much better it is to simply say, "I was wrong. I admit it." Confession truly is good for the soul. Without it, we can never experience forgiveness... which is, after all, the only cure for "burned fingers."

Wash away my pride, Lord, that prevents me
from confessing my wrongdoing.

Thy kingdom is an everlasting kingdom.

Psalms 145:13

◊

In the midst of every ordinary day we can discover evidence of God's kingdom. We find it within us, in faith that dares to believe, in the silent knock of God upon the soul's door. It is present around us, too, in the loving deeds and changed lives of others, as well as nature's quiet, majestic voice. Every day, in countless ways, the kingdom comes.

Give unto the Lord the glory due unto His name.

Psalms 96:8

Have you ever wondered what happened to the cross on which Christ was crucified? Well, there's a legend.

According to this legend, Helen, the mother of Constantine, traveled to Palestine in search of the cross. She looked for it in every corner of the land, and her search turned up not one cross, but three. Helen was unsure. "God," she prayed, "reveal to me which of these crosses is the one on which the Christ King died."

Helen stood the three crosses side by side. One day she noticed a sprig of basil growing from the center cross. Immediately she knew this cross was the real one...for basil comes from the Greek word for king. Helen fell on her knees before the cross with the sweet green basil, in adoration of the King Who had died upon its timbers.

The cross and the basil. A simple legend, but you know, it's a strange thing. The last time I opened my spice cabinet, I remembered that legend. The sweet scent of basil reminded me of the King who hung upon a cross. In the midst of cooking an ordinary meal, I was filled with adoration for the One Who died for me. In the midst of every ordinary day we can all find reminders of this sacrifice.

You are there, Lord, in all the little crannies of our lives.
Today we'll be looking for You.

All things are possible to him that believeth.   Mark 9:23

ot long ago at a backyard picnic, a friend played a little trick on me. When I picked up a new pickle jar and tried to open it, the lid wouldn't budge. So I tried harder, straining at it without luck.

"I can't open this pickle jar. Would you mind loosening it?" I said to Tom.

He took the jar, grunted and groaned as he struggled with the lid, finally handing it back to me. "There you go," he said.

Then, with hardly any effort at all I twisted off the lid as if it were greased. Whereupon Tom began to laugh.

"Sue," he said, "I really didn't do anything to the jar. I only pretended to loosen it."

So there it was again, another example of the tried and true adage: "You can if you think you can."

Keep me aware, Lord, that the first step to believing in myself is believing in You.

And after the fire a still small voice.   I Kings 19:12

I couldn't sleep so I slipped out of bed, pulled on my robe and stepped out onto the porch of the vacation chalet. Snowflakes fell through the darkness, molding the world into a whitened silence. Despite this wintry beauty, my mind returned to the reason for my sleeplessness.

For days I'd been plagued with doubts about my faith. "Oh, God, answer these painful questions. If you are real, if you are here, show me."

My plea drifted up into the night and seemed to vanish. A moment passed. Then something truly wondrous occurred.

As a gentle breeze stirred, I heard music. It seemed to float and twinkle on the air. It was distant, yet near.

Though I saw no one, I knew I was not alone. God was present, filling the night. My doubts evaporated into the freezing air. The wind died and with it the strange heavenly sound.

Sunlight cascaded down the mountains the next morning. I tramped in the snow feeling newly alive, when the wind kicked up and that same haunting music pierced the air. Hanging from a nearby tree was a small and graceful wind chime.

And it is surely true. God moves through our lives like a gentle breeze. And just when we think He is not there at all, if we will only be still and listen carefully, somehow, some way, we will know that He is there.

We are listening for You, Lord.

Nevertheless he saved them for his name's sake, that he might make his mighty power to be known.   Psalms 106:8

So often when I open the newspaper I find myself reading a depressing headline–words in big letters shouting about a world threat, a crisis, another crime. There is surely a lot of bad news to read about these days.

One day I opened our town's paper and read a remarkable headline printed in half-inch letters: "I Asked Jesus Into My Heart." This story followed:

During the night dogs had begun to bark furiously around the home of a local couple. Usually the dogs' barking signaled something amiss, that perhaps prowlers lurked nearby. But the next morning, the couple discovered that nothing had been taken. Instead, something had been returned. Outside the front door were two car speakers that had been stolen six weeks earlier. A note attached to them read, "I'm sorry that I took your speakers, but now I have repented my sins and asked Jesus to forgive me. I hope you will forgive me too. I no longer take other people's belongings...God has changed me. I'm a new creature since I asked Jesus into my heart. From...'Saved'."

God is still alive and at work in the lives of His people, changing them into new and loving creatures. That's not usually front-page news but it's there just the same–tiny happenings in small, unnoticed corners everywhere. So we must not despair when we feel bombarded with bad news. You see, there's a lot of Good News in the world–just waiting to be noticed. Tonight when you sit down with your newspaper or watch the six-o'clock news, you might like to remember that.

You are such Good News, Lord!

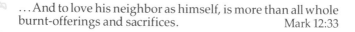

...And to love his neighbor as himself, is more than all whole burnt-offerings and sacrifices.   Mark 12:33

After the Great Fire of London in 1666, the talented architect, Sir Christopher Wren, redesigned most of the churches that had been destroyed. Saint Paul's Cathedral is perhaps the most famous of all. The largest cathedral of the Church of England, it is a magnificent work of architecture that took thirty-five years to build–a towering structure of carvings, columns, arches and spires.

Sir Christopher Wren is buried inside the Cathedral, beneath a plain and simple slab. Barely noticeable and void of trappings, his tomb bears only this inscription: "If you seek his monument, look around you."

Perhaps this is an appropriate epitaph for my life and yours. For most of us, our only monument will be the deeds that we undertake here on earth. Look around you–at what you are doing for loved ones, for your neighbors, for your community.

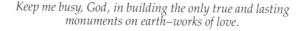

Keep me busy, God, in building the only true and lasting monuments on earth–works of love.

Behold, I stand at the door, and knock: if any man hear My voice, and open the door, I will come in to him, and will sup with him, and he with Me. Revelation 3:20

When I worked as a nurse on the pediatric ward, before I listened to the little ones' chests, I would plug the stethoscope into their ears and let them listen to their own hearts. Their eyes would always light up with awe.

But I never got a response to equal four-year-old David's. I gently tucked the stethoscope in his ears and placed the disk over his heart. "Listen," I said. "What do you suppose that is?"

He drew his eyebrows together in a puzzled line and looked up as if lost in the mystery of the strange tap-tap-tapping deep in his chest. Then his face broke out in a wondrous grin. "Is that Jesus knocking?" he said.

I smiled. Somewhere, maybe in Sunday school, David had obviously been told that lovely old illustration about Jesus standing at the door of our hearts, knocking.

Dear little David. You were exactly right. Inside your heart, and every heart, there is the faint persistent sound of Jesus knocking. For Jesus comes to each of us every new day, wanting to share its moments with us. And maybe it is only those with the faith and wonder of a David who hear it beneath the clamor of a busy world, and open the door.

We're listening, Lord.

Before we went backpacking on the Appalachian Trail, I envisioned all the things that could go wrong out there. I could die from exposure, be eaten by a bear, get lost, fall off a cliff...Needless to say I was overly cautious. I looked for a snake under every rock. I boiled my drinking water in case of contamination. And once, I took a half-mile detour to skirt a rocky ledge.

But despite all the precautions, my trip on the outdoor trail was a disaster. I was finally done in by a wee little half-centimeter blister. I limped along, miserable.

Often I travel the spiritual trail the same way. I stay cautious not to let the big, obvious sins befall me, but overlook the tiny dangers along the way...a small resentment, a tiny lie, a little thread of gossip. And like the blister, it's these lightweight sins that ruin the trip.

Let me be cautious of the small sins, Lord, as well as the big ones. For they are all sins.